LET'S PLAY
GOD'S WAY

MATTHEW HARKER

LET'S PLAY GOD'S WAY

SPORTS AND THE BIBLE

XULON PRESS

Xulon Press
2301 Lucien Way #415
Maitland, FL 32751
407.339.4217
www.xulonpress.com

Paperback ISBN-13: 978-1-66287-075-0
Ebook ISBN-13: 978-1-66287-076-7

ACKNOWLEDGEMENT

I would like to first thank Jesus Christ my Savior for giving me the platform to share his good news of salvation. I also thank God the Father for giving the passion of sports and sending the Spirit which inspired throughout this project, and connecting me with wonderful people that taught, encouraged, prayed for, walked with me, and even given a rebuke when needed.

Garrett Price – Thank you for faithfully walking with God in your sports ministry. Discipling those that you lead to Jesus was what stirred me to start this project. It was an immense pleasure partnering with you.

Andrew George – Thank you for being my "guinea pig" and using these in your Sports ministry while giving me feedback. I pray you don't lose your fire for reaching young men and women athletes.

David Hargrave – Thank you for keeping me accountable and making sure I stay in bounds with context of God's Word. Your encouragement and excitement helped motivate my perseverance to finish.

My Family – Thank you for your patience as I worked on this project. Thank you for your love, support, and all those backyard games we played. I treasure those above any other sports I played.

INTRODUCTION

Welcome to Sports and the Bible. As I read the Bible, I found the stories of competition fascinating. Even Apostle Paul referred to sports that were happening during his time. I wanted to highlight these competitions and show that an athlete or even a general sports fan can have a connection to the God that made us in his image. As an athlete myself, my prayer is that God's Word will be seen in a new and exciting way, through the passion of sports.

Journeying through these 31 shorts readings one can find inspirational quotes, fun sports history, exiting biblical stories, and challenging life applications. A ponder question will help foster introspection and discussion. A prayer at the end will focus readers thoughts toward heaven. This book is not only for an individual devotion but also for a one-on-one discipleship, or a group discussion as each individual lesson is infused with scripture.

Moses wrote,
They are not just idle words for you – they are your life.
Deuteronomy 32:47

Jesus said,
The words that I have spoken to you are spirit and life.
John 6:63

SPORT

"A physical activity requiring skill engaged in for pleasure"

Oksana Baiul – the Ukrainian Olympic Gold Medalist is the only figure skater to win the prestigious Jim Thorpe Inspirational Icon award:

> "One shouldn't be afraid to lose; this is sport. One day you win; another day you lose. Of course, everyone wants to be the best. This is normal. This is what sport is about. This is why I love it."

• • •

Many of the sports we now know today came from everyday life. In every culture around the world throughout history people would pit feats of strength, speed, and cunning against each other. The pride of man would seem to always find a way to make an everyday activity competitive. The imagination of man would create a game then fabricate rules and equipment to utilize if needed. Then in a recreational activity they would gather to find the winner. The earliest records of the Olympics were in 776 BC. A man named Coroebus won the very first event which was an approximate 200-yard sprint.

Let the young men arise and compete before us.–2 Samuel 2:14

One of the most famous competitions in the Bible is the story of David and Goliath found in *1 Samuel 17.* Here we read about a physically average Jewish boy, likely in his teens facing a war seasoned man with a historical recorded height of nine feet tall. David used his weapon of choice, a sling, to beat the heavily armored giant. David told everyone about the God he was taking into the competition. Later he writes "*Blessed be the Jehovah, my rock, who trains my hands for war, and my fingers for battle....*" *(Psa 144:1)* He knew that when he was a shepherd, God was preparing him for this moment by placing a lion, then a bear in his pasture to sharpen his skills. *(1 Sam 17:34-37)*

Even today the analogy of David vs. Goliath is used when an underdog goes against an expected winner. We can learn from David's example of putting in the hard work every day and overcoming the challenges to make us ready for the game ahead. *Whatever you do, work heartily, as for the Lord and not for men, knowing that from Him you will receive the inheritance as your reward.* (Col 2:23) Giving Jehovah God the recognition He deserves for our training because He is *the one who helps you.* (Isa 41:13) *I lift up my eyes... from where does my help come from? My help comes from the LORD, who made heaven and earth.* (Psa 121:1,2)

Ponder: What is the hardest thing you physically do to sharpen your skills?

How about spiritually?

Prayer: Father, help me as I put in the hard work for my sport, school, or work.

Remind me to lift my mind towards you and trust in your help.

ATHLETE

"A person who is proficient in sports and other forms of exercise"

Arthur Ashe – 1st African American tennis player to be rank #1 in the world:

> "You are never really playing an opponent. You are playing yourself, your own highest standards, and when you reach your limits, that is real joy."

• • •

Athletes can range from recreational play to a higher level of competition, to playing for a wage or sponsorship. Natural talent plays a part in an athlete's way in which they can hone skills and rise to the top of the field. Daily devotion to discipline though is the greatest contribution to an athlete's position. One must exercise and train all year to keep the body in shape for a season of play. Studying and analyzing the sport and oneself is also important for education and growth. Let's not forget what every successful athlete has in common… a coach. Someone to teach, train, and push them beyond the limits of what they knew was possible.

> *Every athlete exercises self-control in all things. They do it to receive a perishable wreath, but we do it for imperishable.–1 Corinthians 9:25*

The Bible has examples of feats of athleticism, of strength, of speed, and of skill. It also gives us snippets of characters performing exploits that was important enough to record. The earliest being *mighty men who were of old, the men of renown.* (Gen 6:4) All great deeds in the Bible though have one thing in common; they were all done under the *authority and power given to them* (Luke 9:1,2) by God. It's not to say that the people didn't put the time in sharpening their craft, but when the Almighty ordained the event for His glory and His plan to advance the gospel, then they were taken to heights no one would have imagined.

We always have the opportunity to tap into Jehovah God's power. He can develop us through prayer and His Word on our *speech* and *actions*. He can even give us extraordinary ability if He deems it necessary because *with God all things are possible.* (Matt 19:26) So, whether we go to a local church for a pickup game, or down to the pool for a swim, or *whatever (we) do in word or deed* (Col 3:17) let us not forget to share the good news of Jesus. His promise is that He "*may equip you with all you need for doing his will.*" (Heb 13:21)

Ponder: What do you think extra power or abilities from God would look like?

Prayer: Father, help me to enjoy athleticism through your power. Help me to use it for your purpose.

RULES

"A set of explicit or understood regulations or principles governing a particular activity or sphere"

Lou Holtz – college football national champion head coach with Notre Dame -

> "I follow three rules: Do the right thing, do the best you can, and always show people you care."

• • •

Rules are required in order to decide a winner. They give each sport its individual characteristic separating it as unique. Rules can give the course of route, size of space, length of time, number of players, and how winners are determined. As the sport evolves, the addition and subtraction of rules are needed for the sport to survive. For example, in first year of baseball, the game was played until a team reaches twenty-one runs and only one base was awarded when the ball was hit out of field (i.e., homerun). Furthermore, there were no "called" strikes, only three "swinging" strikes.

> *An athlete is not crowned unless he competes according to the rules. – 2 Timothy 2:5*

Just like an athlete that competes within the rules a Christian must also live within the commandments. Rules in a game are there for order and direction, so it is with a Christian life. Without the commandments there is chaos and confusion. There is a spiritual *warfare* *(Eph 6:12)* for our lives but even the devil must operate within boundaries that God set over him. He is confined to this world *(Eze*

28:17) and cannot harm a God-fearing follower without permission. *(Job 1:11,12)* Jesus kept his first rule simple with two words "*follow me.*" If we adhere that and are "*faithful unto death, (He) will give you the crown of life.*" *(Rev 2:10)*

The commandments of God can be summarized into two, and if we can get these down the rest of the rules will fall into place. The first is *you shall love the Lord your God with all your heart, soul, and mind. And the second is like it: you shall love your neighbor as yourself.* *(Matt 22:37-39)* "Jesus, Others, then You; is a wonderful way to spell J-O-Y," is a child song written by B. Metzger I learned long ago and is a great tool for how God wants me and you to live. Therefore, *do nothing from selfish ambition or conceit, but in humility count others more significant than yourselves. Let each of you look not only to his own interests, but also to the interests of others.* *(Phil 2:3,4)*

Ponder: What is one way you can put others before yourself this week?

Prayer: Father, help me to live within the rules you laid out in order to receive the crown you will give.

ARENA

"Building or enclosure for entertainment or sports.
Syn: field, stadium, pit, gym, rink, park, court"

Wayne Gretzky – Canadian ice hockey player held 61 NHL records in his 20-year career:

> "This is a great arena to play in. The fans are into it. The know their hockey."

• • •

The Colosseum in Rome is the most well-known arena. It was completed under Titus Caesar in 80 AD. It could hold up to 80,000 spectators. It was used for gladiator contests, battle re-enactments, animal hunts, and executions. Such events were performed in smaller, clay and stone floored amphitheaters before. The field in the Colosseum was of dirt and sand; better to soak up blood than the hard grounded amphitheaters. In the arena men had the opportunity to rise as heroes. However, death was the constant occurrence viewed upon by the attendees.

> *Assemble them for battle on the great day of God the Almighty.... And they assembled them at the place that in Hebrew is called Armageddon. –Revelation 16:14,16*

Armageddon is a vast, strategic field used in battles. During the B.C. era it was called the plain of Megiddo. Battles in the past included King Tut in 1469 BC., Joshua and the Israelites in 1405 BC., King Josiah (where he was mortally wounded) in 609 BC., among others. In the future Armageddon will have one last battle between all the armies following the Beast (Anti-Christ), going against Jesus and his army. *They will make war on the Lamb, and the Lamb will conquer them, for he is Lord of lords and King of kings, and those with him are called and chosen and faithful.* (*Rev* 17:14)

Heroes of the faith have conquered and/or died on the grounds of the Arena. Most notably was the Apostle Paul. Historians agree that he was executed in the Colosseum. Paul writes in his last letter just weeks before his death, *For I am already being poured out as a drink offering, and the time of my departure has come. I have fought the good fight, I have finished the race, I have kept the faith.* (2 *Tim* 4:6,7) We like Paul need to pursue heaven as our last field of competition. There we will find the hero's welcome from Jesus, the defeater of death and overcomer of the world, with outstretched arms will say *"well done, good and faithful servant."* (*Matt* 25:23)

Ponder: There is an old saying, "so heavenly minded that they're no earthly good."

Do you believe that is true? Why or why not?

Prayer: Father, I know eternity is real, so help my desire to be with you fuel my walk on earth.

SCORE

"An act of gaining a point, goal, or run in a match or game"

Michael Jordan – six-time NBA champion and a record 10 scoring titles:

> "I want to be perceived as a guy who played his best in all facets, not just scoring. A guy who loved challenges."

• • •

The metric used to evaluate how a game or match is progressing is scoring. Although it is unsure what the first sport to use scoring was, because early matches in history were just win or lose, it is a popular belief that scoring was in place since the existence of team sports. Most sport scoring uses a 1-point metric but there are sports that use unique scoring. American Football and Rugby uses a system based on the type of goal. Tennis uses a 15-to-10-point structure. Bowling uses bonus points, Darts starts at 501 and counts down, and Gymnastics are graded on a scale of ten.

(Love) keeps no record of wrongs.–1 Corinthians 13:5

The relationship between King Saul and David was erratic at best. It went from Saul loving David as his own son and giving him a daughter in marriage, to Saul attempting to kill David on several occasions, taking his wife away from him, and giving her to another man. David did not keep score of the wrongs, or in other word, hold a grudge or have any anger against Saul. In fact, David had two opportunities to harm Saul while he was sleeping but chose not to. He instead told Saul, "*...there is no wrong or treason* *in my hands.... May Jehovah God judge between me and you, may He avenge me against you."* (1 Sam 24:11,12)

God does not want us to hold grudges against anyone. He tells us *do not seek revenge or bear a grudge... but love your neighbor as yourself. I am the Lord."* (Lev 19:18) When we hold a grudge, we are setting ourselves in God's place as judge and avenger. We want to have a sense of control and keeping that record of wrong fulfills that sense. However, being resentful and unwilling to forgive can become like a virus and seep into every relationship we have. There is an old saying "holding a grudge is like drinking poison and hoping the other person dies from it." Instead, we need to *love our enemies. Pray for those that persecute us.* (Matt 5:44) *If they are hungry feed them. If they are thirsty, give them something to drink. In doing this, we will heap burning coals of shame on their heads.* (Rom 12:20)

Ponder: Have you ever held a grudge against someone? What can be done to resolve a grudge?

Prayer: Father, help me to not hold a grudge. It's hard sometimes but I know with your love I can do it.

AWARDS

"A Prize or other mark of recognition given in honor of an achievement"

Jesse Owens – (the Buckeye Bullet) won 4 gold medals at the 1936 Olympic Games in Berlin:

"Awards become corroded; friends gather no dust."

• • •

An olive branch off a wild olive tree only grown in Olympia interwoven in a horseshoe like shape, was the first recorded award giving to the winner of a competition. Today precious medal medallions and unique trophies are the bestowed accolade competitors receive. What started in sports has branched out into areas of life as we find prestigious awards given in humanitarianism (Novel Peace Prize), Entertainment (Oscars), Business (Stevie Award), Food (I.A.C.P. Award), and Military (Medal of Honor, USA), among others.

> *Henceforth there is laid up for me the crown of righteousness, which the Lord, the righteous judge, will award to me on the Day, and not only to me but also to all who have loved his appearing.–2 Timothy 4:8*

Jehovah God rewards those that have trusted in his Son and have lived according to his Word. Jesus did say *"In this world you will have trouble but take heart; I have overcome the world." (John 16:33)* God is looking for finishers, not quitters. He is awarding those that run, walk, or crawl to the finish line. Those that when a mistake in life is made, will look towards heaven, ask forgiveness, and continue on. He is waiting with a crown, not one fashioned to place on the head, but one that will cover the whole being.

The Christian walk is hard. There are so many temptations that will trip us up. Even the Apostle Paul writes *"For I do not understand my own actions. For I do not do what I want, but I do the very thing I hate."* (Rom 7:15) I hate making a derogatory remark towards an opposing player during competition, but I find myself saying it. I must remind myself that it is not the moment of sin that defines me but the whole life I live. For I read that *"the reward for humility and fear of the Lord is riches and honor and life."* (Prov 22:4) Therefore, *let us not become weary in doing good, for at the proper time we will reap a harvest if we do not give up.* (Gal 6:9)

Ponder: What are the things you hate doing that you find yourself doing anyway?

Prayer: Father, help fix the things I hate to do so I can show Jesus more.

EQUIPMENT

"A necessary item or items for a particular purpose"

Mike Krzyzewski (Coach K) – 5-time NCAA basketball championship coach with Duke University:

> "Growing up we made up games. We didn't have equipment. When it snowed, we would play slow motion tackle football. We would play hockey, but we wouldn't skate. We just made things up. I love doing that."

• • •

The majority of sports use some type of equipment; from a simple stick to complex gear with padding and helmet to protect the whole body. Objects used to shoot, catch, or move are common. Shoes are the most utilized piece of equipment. Today shoes are special made for any terrain and ability needed. Balls come in second on the most used sport instrument list. Nevertheless, equipment is essential in any sport. Better the equipment, better the opportunity one has to succeed.

> *Therefore, take up the whole armor of God that you may be able to withstand in the evil day, and having done all, to stand firm.–Ephesians 6:13*

The armor of God has support gear (belt, shoes), protective gear (breastplate, shield, helmet), and offensive gear (sword). Why does a Christian need this equipment? Because they are wrestling against evil *spiritual forces* that has *flaming darts.* *(Eph 6:10-18)* The devil schemes to knock believers in Jesus off the path so they cannot be witnesses. The darts of doubt, self-worth, negativity, and temptation are thrown every day. They are to keep followers from reading the Bible, praying, and telling others about Jesus and what He did for them and what He means to them.

It all starts with the belt; the Belt of Truth as God's Word calls it. Without knowing truth everything else will not be supported. It is like an embarrassing moment when trousers fall to the ankles due to insufficient support. Truth is all of God's words. He can only speak truth. *(Heb 6:18) For the word of the LORD is right and true; he is faithful in all he does. (Psa 33:4)* Not reading the Bible or a devotional daily gives Satan more opportunities to win daily battles. *Watch yourselves, so that you may not lose what you have worked for but may win a full reward. (2 John 1:8)*

Ponder: Do you believe all the Bible is true? If not, what part do you believe is false?

Prayer: Father, help me to put on your armor daily to battle the Devil's darts.

TIME

"The measured or measurable period during which an action, process, or condition exists or continues"

Earl Weaver – A baseball Hall of Fame Major League Manager:

> "You can't sit on a lead and run a few plays into the line and just kill the clock. You've got to throw the ball over the plate and give the other man his chance. That's why baseball is the greatest game of them all."

• • •

Sundial, pendulum, hourglass, water clock, and marked candle kept the time until the mechanical clock appeared in 1200 AD. There is little recorded about time in games until then. Regardless, time is very prevalent and precious in today's sports from the game clock to world records. In some games, time outs are given to help manage the time. Eventually though one constant remains that when the time runs out, its game over.

> *Look carefully then how you walk, not as unwise but as wise, making the best use of the time, because the days are evil.– Ephesians 5:15,16*

To understand the verse above, let us look at first two verses of *Eph 5–1) Therefore, be imitators of God, as beloved children. 2) And walk in love, as Christ loved us and gave himself up for us…* When we complain, worry, delve into things we shouldn't, *or* get angry against someone, we are just wasting time. God says that in making the most of our time we should love and *be kind to one another, tenderhearted, forgiving one another, as God forgave you.* (Eph 4:32) Apostle Paul was in jail when he wrote this. He had every reason to be bitter because he did nothing wrong, but he chose to redeem the time and love his enemy and teach his friends to do the same.

Wasting time is so easy to do. We can do it at school, work, and especially at home. Is wasting time wrong though? It depends on how we value time. God wants us to spend it with him and the people he puts in our lives. He wants us to *build each other up* (Eph 4:29) even during competition. We can even make it a competition when we *outdo one another in showing honor.* (Rom 12:10) When we are at work or school, He wants us to work as if He was our boss. (Col 3:23) If we want to experience real joy, peace, and contentment we need to stop wasting time and start spending it with God.

Ponder: What is one thing we give up today to spend time with God?

Prayer: Father, help me see my day through your plans knowing you have my best interest in mind.

FENCING

"To fight with swords: to practice the art or sport of fencing"

Valentina Vezzali – Italian fencer with six Olympic gold medals and a 16-time World Champion considered the greatest woman fencer of all time:

> "Sport is everything: sort is a metaphor for life. We win and lose, we get up, we start again. Fencing, in particular, teaches you to concentrate more than other sports."

• • •

Competitive fencing started in Egypt more than three thousand years ago. During the reign of Ramses III, an area in the temple was built for sword bouts. During the Roman empire schools were built to train in swordsmanship. Around that same time swordplay was being widely taught as a discipline in the waring China nations of Wu and Yue. Germany and Italy both claim to be founders of the modern fencing which started in the 15th century. The Olympics adopted fencing into the 1896 Athens games and has remained since.

> *Who whet their tongues like swords, who aim bitter words like arrows.–Psalm 64:3*

There are so several stories of sword battles in the Bible. Ehud even made his own sword to use against a king during his time in Judges. In the verse above we read that we can make our own swords by our words. Solomon writes "*...whose rash words are like sword thrust, but the tongue of the wise brings healing.*" *(Prov 12:18)* The words of Solomon are easy to read but hard to do. Try using healing words when being fouled hard during a game. However, James, Jesus' brother, reiterates *"with the tongue we praise our Lord and Father, and with it we curse people that are made in God's image. From the same mouth comes blessing and cursing …this is not right!"* (*James* 3:10)

The Bible says that God's word is also like a sword. *"For the word of God is living and active, shaper than any two-edged sword, cutting between soul and spirit."* (*Heb* 4:12) When we believe what the Bible says is true, that Jesus sacrificed himself for our eternity, then we will be divided from the what the culture says is true. The prince of the world (the devil) will use the culture to separate us from Jesus and God's word, but really *"who can separate us from the love of Christ? Can tribulation, or distress, or persecution, or famine, or nakedness, or danger, or sword?* (*Rom* 8:35) The answer is nothing can.

Ponder: What is things culture says is acceptable, but it's not what God says is acceptable?

Prayer: Father, help me to live my life without compromise yet loving even those that live according to culture.

SHEEP HERDING

"Act of bringing sheep together into a group, maintaining the group, and moving the group from place to place"

Scott Glenn – the Scottish born highlander has won 14 sheep-herding championships and 1 Supreme Championship:

> "Yes, I still get nervous... I think nerves heighten concentration which helps me perform at my best."

• • •

Sheep herding is one of the oldest professions. Sheep will eat a field down to the dirt in a short time. Therefore, they need moved to new grass constantly. Most shepherds have maps that mark feeding locations and order. They also are knowledgeable in weather patterns and are skilled in protecting the flock against predators. Dogs are a herder's best friend and help migrate the sheep to new spots. In 1873 shepherds met in Wales to compete for the "top dog" amongst their peers. The sheep dog competition grew rapidly throughout Europe. In 1928 in made its way to the U.S. where 1,500 attendees gathered to watch the contest.

Now Abel was a keeper of sheep.–Genesis 4:2

The story of Cain and Abel, where Cain kills his younger brother, is still referenced today. *And why did he kill him? Because Cain had been doing what was evil and his brother what was righteous.* (1 John 3:12) See, the brothers took an offering to God. Cain just brought "*fruit of the ground.*" (Gen 4:3) Abel carefully took "*the firstborn of his flock.*" (Gen 4:4) God accepted Abel's offering and did not accept Cain's. So,

Cain *became very angry.* (Gen 4:5) God asked *"why are you angry…? You will be accepted if you do what is right."* (Gen 4:6,7) God wanted the obedience of the heart and Cain just wanted to get by doing his own thing.

The LORD is my shepherd; I shall not want (anymore). He makes me lie down in green pastures. He leads me beside still waters. He restores my soul. (Psa 23:1-3) Jesus is called the good shepherd because *"the good shepherd lays down his life for his sheep."* (John 10:11) Jesus became a willing offering one time for all sins, of all people, of all history and future. All he wants in return is humble obedience of the heart. Sacrifice can be anything from keeping traditions to doing good deeds and is an outward show of faith and can be genuine or faked. God *looks at the heart* (1 Sam 16:7) so *to do righteousness and justice is more acceptable to him than sacrifice.* (Prov 21:3)

Ponder: Is there any traditions, deeds, or activity you can use to show God's love to others?

Prayer: Father, shepherd me away from evil and towards peace.

EQUESTRIAN

"Relating to horse riding. A rider or performer on horseback"

Isabell Werth – most decorated Olympic Equestrian athlete with 6 gold and 4 silver for the German rider:

> "I think the most important quality of an Olympic rider is to have and unswayable belief in the horse you are riding. If you believe in him, you can achieve wonders."

• • •

Horseracing was an event in ancient Greece Olympics in 680 BC. Although historically horses were first used to help cultivate fields and pull carts, evidence of riding began shortly after the Biblical flood. Dressage, an art form of horse riding/dancing for competition, dates to back 1600 AD. It is one of the harder disciplines as it focuses on the harmony between the rider and the horse. Ironically, the sport which started in France made its Olympic debut in the 1900 Paris Olympiad. Eight nations including the United States, participated in four equestrian events.

Harness the horses, mount, O horsemen!–Jeremiah 46:4

Jeremiah, David, and Solomon all write about horses. David and Solomon collected horses. In fact, Solomon at one point had 40,000 stalls for his horses. Jeremiah writes *"If you have raced with men on foot, and have wearied you, how will you compete with horses?"* He expressed the advantage that horses can give. There are cool examples in the Bible of how horses were used, but David says *the war horse is a false hope for salvation, and by its great might, it cannot rescue.* *(Psa 33:17)* Solomon adds *the horse is made ready for the day of battle, but the victory belongs to the Lord.* *(Prov 21:31)*

Another famous biblical horse rider is Jesus. We celebrate one of his rides every Palm Sunday. *They brought it to Jesus, and throwing their cloaks on the colt, they set Jesus on it. And as he rode along, they spread their cloaks on the road.* *(Luke 19:35,36)* As historic as that was, there will be ride from Jesus that the entire world will be witness to. The Apostle John writes *"Then I saw heaven opened, and behold, a white horse! The one sitting on it is called Faithful and True, and in righteousness he judges and makes war."* *(Rev 19:11)* Both rides are that of triumph. One as a humble king and the other as an exulted king. Like the prophetess Deborah's song in *Judges 5* says "the *sound of musicians... repeat the righteous triumph of the LORD,"* let us also repeat the triumphs of Jesus.

Ponder: Nobody but God the Father knows when Jesus' return will be. What are things you can do to prepare for it?

Prayer: Father, give me boldness to share about Jesus so my friends can go with me to heaven.

DARTS

"A sport in which small missiles, pointed on one end and usually feathered on the other, are thrown at a target"

Michael van Gerwen – a Dutch professional darts player from the Netherlands became the youngest to win a PDC World Championship. He also held 8 consecutive world titles:

> "I've always been a positive person. Of course (defeats) upset me, but not for a few days. It affects me a few hours and after that I will be fine again."

• • •

Blow gun darts were found in Mesopotamia as early as 3000 BC. In North America they date back to 1000 BC. They were used not only for hunting but also for warfare. The modern throwing dart was made in France in the 1300's AD. A game of darts was created in the 1400's AD but gained popularity during England's King Henry the 8th's reign, as he was gifted a set of darts on his birthday. The PDC (Professional Darts Corporation) staged the first World Darts Championship in 1994 at the Circus Tavern in Purfleet, Essex.

> *In all circumstances take up the shield faith, with which you can extinguish all the flaming darts of the devil.–Ephesians 6:16*

Satan uses darts to ignite sin such as pride, lust, anger, slander, and gossip. It's his goal to keep people away from being close with God by ruining good character and integrity, because he is the *enemy of all righteousness.* (Acts 13:10) The Devil's greatest weapon is temptation.

If he was bold enough to tempt Jesus *(Matt 4:1-11)* then we are easy targets for him. He was *sinning from the beginning;* (1 John 3:8) he currently *prowls around like a lion* (1 Pet 5:8) dragging whomever he can with him because he knows his fate is the lake of fire where he *will be tormented day and night forever and ever.* *(Rev 20:10)*

God doesn't leave us on our own to deal with Satan. He tells us to *give no opportunity to the devil* (Eph 4:27) by *submitting ourselves to God.* (James 4:7) Being watchful and alert towards recognizing the devil's tricks will help us to resist him. The shield of faith is a powerful tool in our stand against the evil one. See faith is the confidence that things will happen, and the guarantee that the unseen is true. *If you are not firm in faith, you will not be firm at all.* *(Isa 7:9)* So *be watchful, stand firm in the faith, act like men, be courageous, be strong,* (1 Cor 16:13) *watch, and pray so that you will not fall into temptation.* *(Matt 26:41)*

Ponder: What are temptations you that pull you away from God?

Prayer: Father, teach me to identify temptations and train me to resist them.

ARCHERY

"The skill, practice, or sport of using a bow to shoot arrows, especially at a target"

Kim Soo-Nyung – the South Korean is the most decorated female archer in Olympic history with 4 golds, a silver, and a bronze:

> "Archery gives you conviction. People need conviction all the time: to eat well, to do anything well."

• • •

The Bow and Arrow was fabricated as a way to launch a projectile faster than it could be thrown. Although the exact origin is not known cave drawings as early as 3000 BC reveal hunters using the bow. In China, archery dates to the Shang Dynasty – 1766-1027 BC. The first recorded archery competition was 1583 AD in England. The Olympic Organization held its first archery event in the year 1900 AD. Hubert Van Innis of Belgium won the first gold. When he retired, he accumulated six gold and three silver medals making him the most successful archer in the history of the Olympic games.

> *He lived in the wilderness and became and expert with the bow.–Genesis 21:20*

This verse describes Ishmael the son of Abraham. Ishmael's life was not easy. He was sent away by his father, raised by his mother, and lived in a desert region. Abraham loved his first-born son though and was *distressed greatly* *(Gen 21:11)* when Ishmael left. However, *God was with* Ishmael. *(Gen 21:20)* God also promised to make him into *a great nation.* (Gen 21:18) God did just that as Ishmael went on to having twelve sons and became the founding father of the Arab religion. When Abraham died, Ishmael was there helping his half-brother Isaac bury the father they both loved. (Gen 25:9)

In the story of Ishmael and his mother Hagar, God met them in the wilderness after they were sent away. God heard their cries and came to the rescue. (Gen 21:17) God loves the outcast and the down and out that cry out to Him. Ishmael in Hebrew means "God hears." God is always available whenever we need to talk to him as he never *slumbers nor sleeps* (Psa 121:4) and will *attend to the voice of our prayer.* (Psa 66:19) He declares, *"my eyes will be open and my ears attentive to the prayer that is made."* (2 Chron 7:16) *"Call upon me and come pray to me, and I will hear you."* (Jer 29:12) Furthermore, if we make a request according to His will, *he will give us what we ask for.* (1 John 5:14,15)

Ponder: Knowing that God hears prayers, does that give you more confidence to pray? Where are unusual places you have prayed?

Prayer: Father, help me to come to you more often knowing that you are always there.

JAVELIN

"A light spear thrown in a competitive sport or as a weapon"

Neeraj Chopra – Javelin thrower and first Track and Field athlete to win a gold medal for India:

> "I think more and more kids will see what we're achieving and be inspired to pick up a javelin in themselves"

• • •

The difference between a javelin and a spear was the javelin was shorter and lighter weight and could be thrown for a greater distance. They were more widely used in northern Europe. The javelin throw became part of the pentathlon in the 708 BC Olympic Games. Centuries after the Greece Olympic games ended in 394 AD, Finland and Sweden revived the sport in the late 1700s. Target throw and distance throw were the two javelin events; however, the distance throw became much more popular and target throwing was ultimately dropped. The javelin throw made its way back into the Olympics in 1908. A Swede named Eric Lemming dominated the sport for decades. In 1932 American Babe Didrikson won the inaugural Olympic women's javelin throw.

> *Clubs are counted as stubble; he laughs at the rattle of javelins.–Job 41:29*

In this chapter of Job, God recounts his creation of the Leviathan. The Leviathan was a large serpent like sea creature that according to Jewish tradition, was created on the fifth day when *God created the great sea creatures.* *(Gen 1:21)* Over 200 times creation is referred to in the Bible. It is an important foundation for the Jewish and Christian faith. Creation is the only life origin account that does not have any chaos, destruction, or death. The six days of creation were pure and perfect and God's first show of his great love towards us. *"The heavens declare the glory of God, and the sky proclaims his handiwork."* *(Psa 19:1)*

Creation gives the answers humans have sought throughout history; Who am I? Why am I here? *God created (us) in his own image.* *(Gen 1:27)* God goes on to say, *"Before I formed you in the womb, I knew you.* *(Jer 1:5)* *"I call you by your name. I named you, though you do not know me."* *(Isa 45:4)* *Why, even the hairs of your head are all numbered.* *(Luke 12:7)* God's intimate knowledge of us fuels His desire for a relationship with us. We are God's creation and can be his cherished son or daughter if we *believe in his name.* *(John 1:12)* We are here because we are *created for his glory, whom he formed and made.* *(Isa 43:7)* We exclaim his renown, spread his fame, show his excellence. We are here to do *good works which God prepared beforehand.* *(Eph 2:10)* We are *a people for his own possession, the (we) may proclaim the excellencies of him who called (us) out of darkness into his marvelous light.* *(1 Peter 2:9)*

Ponder: Because we are made in the image of God, what are ways we are like Him?

Prayer: Father, help me become more intimate with you sharing things I've never told anyone.

SWIMMING

"The sport or activity of propelling through water using the limbs, fins, or tail"

Michael Phelps II – U.S. swimmer and most decorated Olympian of all time with 28 total medals:

> "I think the biggest things I am looking forward to is getting new faces in the sport. Getting kids who could be afraid of the water to feel comfortable in the pool."

• • •

Swimming dates to as far as the first boats. Makes sense that if someone is a seafarer then they should know how to swim. Romans in the 1st century BC built swimming pools that were separate from millennia old, multicultural bathing pools. They used the pools to for military training. The first swimming competition was held in Australia in 1846. In 1896 the Olympics held men's swimming races, then in 1912 added women's swim events.

> *And (God) will spread out is hands in the midst of it as a swimmer spreads his hands out to swim.–Isaiah 25:11*

There is a prophecy in *Isaiah chapter* 25 that one day there will be rest, and a feast, and rejoicing... basically a big party with a *great multitude which no one could number, of all nations, tribes, peoples, and languages, standing before the throne and before the Lamb. (Rev 7:9,10)* God will *make a feast of rich food, a banquet of aged wine..., and he will swallow up death forever; and he wipe away tears from all faces. (Isa 25:8)* This is all made possible because Jesus spread his hands out alone on the cross just like a swimmer would do to propel through the water. This is just one of several times the Bible talks about life in heaven. It will be glorious!

Jesus went off to pray and was transfigured, that is transformed into something much more elevated and beautiful. He had a meeting with Moses and Elijah as was witnessed and recognized by Peter, James, and John. Later Jesus was beaten badly and nailed to a cross and died, but after he rose from death, he was seen in a glorious form but still had his scars. The Bible doesn't answer all the questions such as those that lose limbs on earth, but we do know our heavenly bodies will be beautiful, limitless, and elevated by God *who will transform our lowly body to be like His glorious body.* *(Phil 3:21)* *"For I consider that the sufferings of this present time are not worthy to be compared with the glory which shall be revealed in us."* *(Rom 8:18)*

Ponder: What do you think heaven will be like?

Prayer: Father, thank you for making a place where no more pain or sorrow will exist. A place of beauty and wonder, where our new bodies can live with you.

THE BALL

"A solid or hollow sphere or ovoid, especially one that is kicked, thrown, or hit in a game"

Pele' – 3-time FIFA gold medalist and voted FIFA player of the 20th century:

> "You must respect and work hard to be in shape. And I used to train very hard. When other players went to the beach after training, I was there kicking the ball."

• • •

Archaeology has uncovered a ball being used in sports as early as 1600bc. Almost every culture has used a ball in its games, like soccer style *cuju* in China to a field hockey type game *genna* in Ethiopia. *Episkyros* was a rugby/American football kind of sport played in Greece. However, the oldest culture that was uncovered to use a ball was Mesoamerica (currently Central America) which played a game similar to volleyball called *Ollamaliztli.*

> *Behold, Jehovah will hurl you away violently, O you strong man. He will seize firm hold on you and whirl you around and around and throw you like a ball into a wide land.– Isaiah 22:17,18*

Ball is only mentioned once in the Bible. Isaiah uses it in a prophecy written around 730 BC. He is writing to Israel. Here the leaders and people of Israel think they are the strongest nation. They don't want God's help. In fact, they totally ignored and even persecuted the men and women God uses to tell them to turn back to Him.

The Apostle Paul later asks, *"which of the prophets did your ancestors not persecute?"* (Acts 7:52) So, God inspires Isaiah to use an object widely known to give warning that *whoever is not with me is against me.* (Matt 12:30)

When I look at great sports personalities, I often wonder what their thoughts are about Jesus. I see people succeeding in place they have trained hard for. It is when I investigate their life story, I find either humility, giving God the glory for some, or arrogance, saying they did it on their own for others. It is that second group that confuses me. God gave them their body, ability, and put people in their lives to help them get to where they are at. God not only wants us to give *praise that is due him* (Psa 65:1) but also those that helped us. *Do not withhold good from those to whom it is due, when it is in your power to do it.* (Prov 3:27) *Behold God is my helper, the Lord is the upholder of my life.* (Psa 54:4)

Ponder: Would you want to be successful with God or a success without God? Why?

Prayer: Father, help me to give you credit in everything. Remind me to thank all the people you put in my life to help me.

SLINGING

"A simple weapon in the form of a strap or loop, used to hurl stones or other small missiles"

Israelmore Ayivor – Inspirational writer and speaker from Ghana, for youth and leadership:

> "If God's will be in your little stones, they will surely bring down giant Goliaths. But you have to make the throw."

• • •

Historians consider the sling to be the first projectile weapon. A slings projectile can have a greater velocity than that of an arrow shot by a compound bow, although the arrow is deadlier at a greater distance. Slings were a common weapon widely used. They were found in the tomb of King Tutankhamen (Tut), with the "barbarians" of early Russia, and also the early Americas. The oldest sling artifact was found in Peru and dated to approximately 2500 B.C. The greatest invading armies such as the Greek and Romans by land, and Vikings and Spain by sea feared the sling more than any other weapon. Target slinging was an event in the Greek Olympics. Coins were discovered that depict an Olympic slinger give evidence to the competition.

> *Among all these were 700 chosen men who were left-handed; everyone could sling a stone at a hare and not miss. – Judges 20:16*

The skilled warriors that were amazing slingers were a community from the tribe of Benjamin that had a dark side. To set the stage *in those days there was no king in Israel. Everyone did what was right in his own eyes.* (Judg 21:25) This particular town did something so atrocious that it changed the future of Israel. The story of *Judges 19-21* is a big warning to us about an unloving relationship and sexual impurity. The sin in the home of the Levite escalated events to wickedness unimaginable such as rape, murder, body mutilation, and almost an annihilation of a whole tribe. Disregarded the ten commandments and God's way to live a life of peace and joy not only effected the individuals directly involved but the whole nation.

God gave us stories about what happens when we abandon the way He set up sexual relationships. *God's will is that you should be (consecrated and pure): that you should avoid sexual immorality; that each of you should learn to control their own body in a way that is holy and honorable, not in passionate lust… for God did not call us to be impure, but to live a holy life.* (1 Thes 4:3-5,7) *Do you not know that your body is a temple of the Holy Spirit who is in you…?* (1 Cor 6:19) When we live by God's established instructions for purity before marriage, we avoid negative entanglements that affect us and those around us. Moreover, keeping marriages pure where there is unashamed sex and unreserved love that God intended, can quite possibly heal a nation hurting from so many broken relationships.

Ponder: What are lustful or sexual temptations that Satan uses to trip you?

Prayer: Father, starting today help me to keep my body pure in my relationship with you and my spouse, current or future.

COACH

"An athletic instructor or trainer;
a tutor who gives specialized training"

Glen Mills – the Jamaican coach is one of the top track coaches of all time:

> "My knowledge is not exclusive as I believe that other people have similar information. We all get it from the same research, the same scientific data, but maybe I can use it better than most."

• • •

Greek historian Plutarch wrote about the training regimen the Spartan boys went through back in 400 BC. The trainers who were seasoned veterans, gave them a strict diet, only one cloak to wear, and trained them on every terrain and in all-weather environments. They are known as having one of the greatest militaries in history all do to the strict, intense training stricture that was in place. Like the Spartans of old, today's athlete relies on their coach for continual improvement. Though numerous sports allow the coach with the athlete when performing, and some don't, the coach is ever-present.

> *Remember your leaders, those who spoke to you the word of God.–Hebrews 13:7*

There are examples of an older more experienced person training up one that is willing to listen and learn. Eli and Samuel, Elijah and Elisha, Moses and Joshua, and the most famous, Jesus and the Disciples are a handful that comes to mind. In each example the mentor teaches the trainees the ways in which they need to *act justly, love mercy, and walk humbly with God.* (*Micah* 6:8) The apprentices then became strong leaders themselves carrying with them the wisdom given by their mentors. *A disciple is not above his teacher, but when fully trained will be like his teacher* (*Luke* 6:40)

The apostle Paul and Timothy is another example of a teacher and student. Paul met the young man on his second missionary journey and trained him to be a leader of himself. Paul saw his potential and desire to succeed in spreading the gospel and poured his time and knowledge into him. After Paul sent Timothy out, he gave the advice, *don't let anyone look down on you because you are young, but set an example for believers in speech, in conduct, in love, in faith and in purity.* (1 *Tim* 4:12) With the right teaching the young, old, the outcast, the handicapped, and the autistic can go on to inspire their world, and even sports to *the glory of the Father in heaven.* (*Phi* 2:11)

Ponder: The second part of *Hebrews 13:7* is "*Consider the outcome of their way of life and imitate their faith.*" Is there a godly man or woman in your life whose faith you can imitate?

Prayer: Father, help me humble myself to be coached so I can grow stronger for you.

DANCING

"An activity of moving one's feet or body, or both,
for pleasure and to entertain others"

Tessa Virtue and Canadian partner Scott Moir – with 3 Ice Dancing gold medals has become the most decorated Ice Dance team of all time:

"Flawless' is an unattainable thing."

• • •

Ice dancing, synchronized swimming, and rhythmic dancing are all a form of competitive dancing in the Olympics that came in the 1900's. In 2018 break dancing made its debut in the Buenos Aires Youth Olympics and added to the Paris 2024 Olympic program. Dancers are scored on creativity, personality, technique, variety, performativity, and musicality on three elements – top rock, down rock, and freeze.

David danced before the Lord with all his might.–2 Samuel 6:14

King David loved to dance as the verse above shows. He encouraged others to dance with writings like, "*let them praise his name with dancing.*" (*Psa 149:3*) He inspired others to dance also as we read, "*Is not this David, of whom they sing to one another in dances.*" (*1 Sam 29:5*) He uses dancing as an act of worship. "*You turned my mourning into dancing... that my glory may sing your praise and not be silent.*" (*Psa 30:11,12*) Solomon, David's son, reminds us that there is a *time to dance.* (*Ecc 3:4*) When Jesus permanently everyone will *go forth to the dances of the merrymakers.* (*Jer 31:4*)

Worship is more than attending church and singing songs on Sunday. It is something one lives for, strives for, every waking moment. Webster's Dictionary defines worship as "to honor or show reverence for a divine being." We know this divine being as the *Living God.* (1 Sam 17:26) Living every day by respecting and following the bible worships Jehovah God. God honors the dedication as example is *Acts 2:46,47 "every day they continued to meet together. They broke bread in their homes and ate together with glad and sincere hearts, praising God and enjoying the favor of all the people. And the Lord added to their number daily those who were being saved.* Dancing, singing, playing instruments, authoring books, cooking, sharing meals, raising children, and even playing sports can be an outward act of a dedicated daily living and worship.

Ponder: What are the things you live for or strive for? Is Jesus among them?

Prayer: Father help me to remember you daily so I can focus my worship on you.

FISHING

"Activity of catching fish, either for food or as a sport"

Ernest Hemingway – 1954 Nobel Prize winner was an avid fisherman and started the Earnest Hemingway Bill-fishing Tournament in Cuba back in 1950 and still going on every year:

> "Perhaps I should not have been a fisherman... But that was the thing that I was born for." (*From the book Old Man and the Sea)*

• • •

The earliest fishing picture was found in Egypt and dated for 2000 BC. It is widely believed that fishing predates that as the early civilizations that lived near rivers and lakes fished as a main source of food. The early fishhook was made from a small piece of wood or bone filed to sharp at both ends. Bronze fishhooks became widely popular during the Bronze Age in 3000 BC. Today the largest fishing competition is Bisbee's Black and Blue Marlin Tournament where the prize money is in the millions.

> *Go to the sea and cast a hook and take the first fish that comes up, and when you open its mouth, you will find a shekel.– Matthew 17:27*

There are great stories involving fish as the events in the Bible took place around the Mediterranean region. Stories such as Jonah and the great fish, Job describing the mighty leviathan, Peter and Andrew hulling in so many fish the boat almost sank. But the one that always stood out for me was the fish and the shekel. Peter and

Jesus were approached about paying the yearly temple tax which a miracle provided. Later Jesus was confronted about paying taxes and he responded "*...give to Caesar the things that are Caesar's, and to God the things that are God's.*" (Matt 22:21)

What are the things of God's? Time spent to grow a relationship with God. Talents, such as teaching, or athletics used to glorify God. Thoughts, being on things that are honorable, pure, and just. (*Phil* 4:8) Trust, that God always knows what's best for us and blesses us accordingly. Treasures are all the monetary and material things we have that can be used to spread the love of Jesus. That last one comes with comes with at challenge and a promise; "*Bring the tithe into the storehouse, that there may be food in my house. Test me in this" says God Almighty, "and see if I will not throw open the floodgates of heaven and pour out so much blessing that there will not be enough to store it.*" (*Malachi* 3:10) In all areas of our life we *must decide in (our) heart how much to give. And don't give reluctantly or in response to pressure. For God loves a cheerful giver.*" (2 Cor 9:7)

Ponder: How can I use my treasure to God fulfill his plans?

Prayer: Father, help me to give my time, talents, thoughts, treasures, and trust cheerfully so that so that you can be honored.

HUNTING

"Activity or sport of chasing or searching for wild animals or birds with the intention of catching or killing"

Jim Thorpe – Native American athlete that won 2 Olympic Gold medals in pentathlon and decathlon, afterwards he played professional Baseball, Football, and Basketball:

"My favorite sport is hunting and fishing."

• • •

In the early civilizations the hunters were the upper-class citizens. They used spears, darts, arrows, nets, and traps to provide food, clothing, and tools. During the Roman empire though the nobility viewed hunting as beneath them and allocated it to underlings. One of the most famous hunters in history, John George II of Saxony shot a total of 42,649 deer. Not to be left out, European women became known as expert hunters, such as Maria Governess of the Netherlands, with crossbow would track, kill, and gut stags. Also, Elizabeth 1st was known for her hunting and hawking skills.

(Nimrod) was a mighty hunter before the Lord.–Genesis 10:9

Nimrod was the first hunter mention in the Bible, but Esau son of Isaac and Jacob's twin brother was a great hunter also. Esau was robust, warmhearted, and yet a sometimes-impulsive man that loved his father and would do anything for him. The reason Jehovah God chose Jacob over Esau was because Esau relied solely on his skill to get him through life and didn't have time for God. Even though Esau made poor choices he still loved his family. After years of being separated from his brother Jacob, upon seeing him *Esau ran to meet him and embraced him and fell on his neck and kissed him, and they wept.* (Gen 33:4) Esau had every reason to be angry with the brother that deceived and stole his birthright and blessing but chose love instead.

To most athletes, family is especially important. They are most times the greatest cheerleaders, comforters, supporters, and motivators. But sometimes in a family an offense happens between members and hurt will run deep. Who can hurt you more than the one you love the most, right? What seems unforgivable is never unforgivable. We need to forgive and love and seek to be *eager to maintain unity of the Spirit in the bond of peace.* (Eph 4:3) A strong family in unity will be a bright light of hope that the world is drawn to. *Whoever loves his brother (family) abides in the light, and in him there is no cause for stumbling.* (1 John 2:10)

Ponder: What can you do to help your family grow stronger together?

Prayer: Father, help me forgive and love my family as you love your family.

WEIGHTLIFTING

"The act, art, or sport of lifting barbells as conditioning or competitive event"

Zydrunas Savickas (Big Z) – a Lithuanian powerlifter that has won 4 World Strong Man Championships, 8 Arnold Strongman Classics, and is considered one of the greatest of all strongmen:

> "It's a lot of pain, basically: legs, back, hands, shoulders. All sports, they are mostly about pain and being able to overcome."

• • •

Cave drawings have depicted men lifting large rocks as a feat of strength. As far back as 3500 BC Egypt, Mesopotamia, and China had lifting regiments for their armies. Dumbbells first appeared in Greece. They were distinct size stones with handles carved into them. Families in Scotland would have a giant rock to lift as a rite of passage for a boy to become a man. In 1896 a revived Olympic game included weightlifting as an event. Today there are ten weightlifting medal events – five for men and five for women.

> *As Moses lifted up the serpent in the wilderness, so must the Son of Man be lifted up.–John 3:14*

The people of Israel needed physical healing, so God told Moses to *make a fiery serpent and set it on a pole* (Num 21:8), and whoever looked at it was healed. Jesus used that image to explain what was going to happen to him, *"and I, when I am lifted up from the earth, will draw all people to myself."* (John 12:32) That became true when *he was pierced for our rebellion, crushed for our sins. He was beaten so we could be whole. He was whipped so we could be healed.* (Isa 53:5) He did that for us, his *friends* (John 15:14) because he wants to lift us *out of darkness into his marvelous light.* (1 Peter 2:9)

Fellowship is a partnership with one or more friends along life's journey. Friends can help us grow stronger, not only physically but emotionally and spiritually also. *Two are better than one..., if either of them falls, one can help the other up. Three are even better for a triple-braided cord is not easily broken.* (Ecc 4:10-12) *Friends give pleasant, sincere advice, seeking our highest good.* (Prov 27:9) Don't do life alone. Make lifting one another up, praying for one another, and encouraging each other a part of your daily routine. *Above all, love each other deeply, because love covers a multitude of sins.* (1 Peter 4:8)

Ponder: Who can you pray for or encourage today?

Prayer: Father, help my friend or family member today as they go through hard things.

RACING

"A competition of speed; operate at excessive speed; beat faster (as one's heart)"

Mario Andretti – Italian-born American racing driver was one of the most successful in the history of motorsports by winning in Formula One, IndyCar, World Sportscar, and NASCAR:

> "If everything seems under control, you're not going fast enough."

• • •

Most racing games were derived from religious festivals. The earlies recorded racing competition took place in Ireland. As part of the Tailteann games which was held in 829 BC, which predates the first Olympic games in 776 BC. The local Gaelic folklore claims the first race dates to 1600 BC. They were held in northeast Ireland near Teltown in County Meath. The games did not only consist of contests of speed like racing, strength like wrestling, and skill like archery, they also had contests of singing, storytelling, dancing, goldsmithing, weaving, and strategy.

The chariots race madly through the streets.–Nahum 2:4

The city of Nineveh was the capital of Assyria. Around one hundred years before Nahum, God sent the prophet Jonah to tell of God's mercy, which the Ninevites accepted. However, it did not last long, and the Assyrians became a very wicked nation oppressing the kingdoms they conquered and performing evil acts on the people. Nahum wrote about the judgement coming which the armies and chariots of the Babylonians enacted 50 years later. Nahum explained the *"the LORD is a jealous and avenging God... He is slow to anger and great in power, and by no means lets the guilty go unpunished."* (Nahum 1:1,2)

Assyrians could have done good for the world but instead turned to abuse their power and abuse the people. Abuse can happen anywhere: home, sports, online; and does not only come in physical form such as beatings or molestation, but also in psychological or emotional such as neglect, shaming, or rendering guilt. We can find most of these exampled in *1 John* which the apostle John writes *"is not from the Father but is from the world."* Victims of abuse want their hurt repaired by the abuser taking responsibility and making amends, but sadly that will not happen. But God can *heal the brokenhearted* (Psa 147:3) and urges to *cast all anxieties on him, because he cares.* (1 Peter 5:7) His *steadfast love never ceases, and his mercies never end* (Lam 3:22), *because* He is *the Father of mercies and the God of all comfort, who comforts us in all our affliction.* (2 Cor 1:3:4)

Ponder: What insecurities do you have that makes you question your value?

Prayer: Father, heal my hurts and show me that I am worthy enough to be a part of your family.

WRESTLING

"Contend by grappling with and striving to trip or throw an opponent down or off balance"

Alexander Medved – the Soviet Union athlete is one of the greatest Olympic wresters of all time:

> "In order to become a wrestler, one should have the strength of a weightlifter, the agility of an acrobat, the endurance of a runner, and the tactical mind of a chess master."

• • •

Uncovered art in Babylon depicts wrestlers engaging in their sport as early as 3000 BC. They seem to be using what today is called belt wrestling, in which combatants wear a special belt, use hold, and throw to take their opponent to the ground. In 776 BC wrestling became part of the Olympics in Greece. When modern day Olympics began in 1896 in Athens, a German named Carl Schuhmann won the gold in Greco-Roman style wrestling in which no leg take downs are permitted. Freestyle wrestling, which allows leg take downs, made its Olympic debut in 1904.

> *Jacob was left alone, and a man wrestled with him.– Genesis 32:24*

Jacob wrestled not in the physical but in the spiritual. He was about to meet his brother Esau for the first time after stealing his first-born blessing. Jacob spent the night in prayer. The Son of God which often appeared in a form similar to an angel, came to Jacob. Jacob wrestled with him with conversation through prayer and said,

"I will not let you go unless you bless me." (Gen 32:26) It was then that God said to Jacob, *"from now on you will be called Israel, because you have fought with God and with men and have won."* (Gen 32:28) Once a coward that stole a blessing, Jacob was now a warrior that courageously stood firm in faith and prayer for a greater blessing.

Paul, as he often did, uses a sport to emphasize a spiritual discipline as he writes *"For we do not wrestle against flesh and blood, but... against spiritual forces of evil in the heavenly places."* (Eph 6:12) Paul knew the only way to fight against the unseen was through prayer. He urges us *to pray without ceasing* (1 Thes 5:17), and *to not be anxious about anything* (Phili 4:6) *praying at all times in the Spirit.* (Eph 6:18) Here is a super cool thing, the Spirit helps us! *For we do not know what to pray for as we ought, but the Spirit himself intercedes for us with groanings too deep for words.* (Rom 8:26) Talk about a powerful tag team.

Ponder: What are tactics that Satan uses to keep you from praying?

Prayer: Father, I know praying is just talking to you, help me to continually pray whether out loud or in my thoughts.

HIGH JUMP

"An athletic event in which competitors jump over a bar placed at measured heights without dislodging it"

Javier Sotomayor – Cuban High Jumper and only person to clear over 8 feet:

> "If someone breaks my record, I will not celebrate it. I will accept it. I will go to them, shake their hand, and congratulate them."

• • •

In 1948 doctor Sir Ludwig Guttman, outside of London England wanted to help paraplegic World War II veterans with rehabilitation and started Olympic style events for them to compete in. In 1960 the first official Paralympic Games were held with 23 countries and 400 athletes in attendance. Chicago's Soldier Field in 1968 held the first Special Olympics. Eunice Kennedy Shriver a champion for the rights of people with intellectual disabilities founded the events when she seen how unfairly they were left out. Today there are over six million athletes from over 190 countries and territories with more than one million coaches and volunteers that participate in the Special Olympics. Rules are modified in events like the high jump, long jump, shot put, discus, and other events to accommodate the athletes.

"By my God I can leap over a wall."–2 Samuel 22:30

The chapter of 2 Samuel 22 is titled the Song of Deliverance. It reflects all the time God had David's back and gave him extra prowess. He goes on to write *"The LORD dealt with me according to my righteousness."* (2 Sam 22:21) As I look back at David's life the story of Mephibosheth shows me kindness and righteousness of David's heart. Mephibosheth was Jonathan's son and crippled in both legs. After King Saul and Jonathan died in the same battle David brought Mephibosheth into his home. He told Mephibosheth *"I will show you kindness for the sake of your father Jonathan, and I will restore to you all the land of Saul, and you shall eat at my table always."* (2 Sam 9:7,8)

Today when I think of a champion for the people with disabilities Joni Eareckson Tada comes to mind every time. Joni is paralyzed from the neck down due to a diving accident. She is the founder of Joni and Friends, and their goal is to "help someone with a disability find hope, dignity, and their place in the body of Christ." (joniandfriends.org) God blesses her ministry because he too champions for those with disabilities. In *Duet 27:18* God warns, *"Cursed is anyone who leads a blind person astray… and all the people will reply 'Amen'."* Jesus took time to heal those with disabilities. He proposes, *"when you give a banquet, make it your habit to invite the poor, the cripple, the lame, and the blind. Then you will be blessed…. And you will be repaid when the righteous are resurrected."* (Luke 14:14)

Ponder: Is there anyone with disabilities that you cross paths with? What can you do to encourage them?

Prayer: Father, help me see everyone as you see them.

ANIMAL FIGHTING

"Combat between two or more animals, or human and animal, for livelihood, sport, or entertainment"

Manuel Rodriguez Sanchez "Manolete" – Spain's greatest bull fighter of all time:

> "It's not about what you do on a good day. It's what you do on a bad day."

• • •

Allegator wrestling, bullfighting, and even octopus wrestling are types of man verses animal competition. From the beginning of time people had to fight wild animals for survival. Earliest recordings of dogs used in battle was 700 BC. Though they were domesticated long before that. Also around that time was the first recorded bull fight around the region of Spain. In 500 BC. Romans began to pit man in combat against lions, elephants, bulls, and tigers in arenas for sport.

> *And Benaiah the son of Jehoiada a valiant man… struck down a lion in a pit on a day when snow had fallen.–2 Samuel 23:20*

Samson, David, Elisha, and Daniel are just a few with stories of run-ins against fierce animals. I chose Benaiah because he was one of King David's trusted friends. David surrounded himself with people of like mind. They were thirty warriors and served Jehovah God. Three of them became David's truest confidants. (2 Sam 23:1) The team assisted in making David into one of the greatest kings in history. David would even pray for his team, "*for my brothers and companions' sake I will say, 'Peace be within you!'*" (Psa 122:8)

Like David we need to surround ourselves with people that have the same spiritual beliefs as our own. Proverbs 27:17 states "*Iron sharpens iron, and one man sharpens another.*" We are already surrounded by warriors in our sport to sharpen our skill, having one or more around us to keep our walk in the Spirit sharp will in essence boost readiness in every aspect of our lives. Even better is to have a friend that is open and honest giving advice because *the sweetness of a friend comes from his earnest counsel.* (Prov 27:9) Also someone that isn't afraid to challenge our harmful actions because *wounds from a friend can be trusted.* (Prov 27:6) So, *walk with the wise and become wise* (Prov 13:20) and *prevail with great power.* (Prov 24:5)

Ponder: Do you have friend or adult that will keep you spiritually sharp?

Will you allow them to?

Prayer: Father, help me to be open to feedback spiritually and physically, so I can grow in both.

ROCK CLIMBING

"Activity or sport in which participants climb up, down, or across natural rock formations or artificial rock walls"

Adam Ondra – Czech professional rock climber, considered the best in the world at lead climbing and bouldering:

> "I think climbing deserves to be an Olympic sport, as it is one of the few natural movements – like swimming or running. Things that people have been doing for a thousand years."

• • •

The earliest records of rock climbing were found in the Alpine area of Northern Europe. People would climb to reach eggs for food, mine minerals, and escape enemies. Throughout history there are noted battles where cliffs, peaks, or walls were needed to climb to lay siege on a castle or reach an opposing army. It wasn't till the 1800's AD that rock climbing was used as a sport. England, Germany, France, and Italy all started competitive groups during that time. In 1886 England's Walter Parry Haskett Smith made the first solo climb and inspired a new era of climbing. By 1930 there were over two hundred climbing clubs. In the 2020 Olympics, Sport Climbing became a medal event in which Alberto Gines of Spain took gold and Nathaniel Coleman of U.S.A took silver.

> *Jonathan said to his armor-bearer, "Climb up after me..." Jonathan climbed using his hands and feet.–1 Samuel 14:12,13*

This story of Jonathan will tell of an incredible feat of strength and devotion to Jehovah God. Jonathan and his armor bearer were between two rocky crags. The enemy was atop of one braggingly shouting, *"look they are crawling out of their holes... Come up and we will teach you a lesson."* *(1 Sam 14:12)* Jonathan totally dependent on God humbly exclaimed, *"God will act on our behalf. Nothing can hinder the LORD from saving."* *(1 Sam 14:6)* The two men then climbed the rocky cliff and immediately battled a garrison of soldiers.

I wonder if the story would have turned out differently if Jonathan boasted in his own strength? Knowing that his own physical abilities could make the climb and then swing a sword could have stroked his ego. Yet he demonstrated that *pride leads to disgrace, but with humility comes wisdom.* *(Prov 11:2)* God has boundless strength and wants us to set aside our conceit, bragging, and self-pride and lean on Him. *"Don't let the wise boast in their wisdom or the strong boast of their strength or the rich boast of their riches, but let the one boast in this, that they understand and knows me, that I am God who practices steadfast love, justice, and righteousness in the earth. For in these things I delight, declares Jehovah."* *(Jer 9:23,24)*

Ponder: How does one brag before, during, or after a game? When does bragging go too far?

Prayer: Father, it is hard not to brag about my abilities and accomplishments. Remind me to brag about you, the one that gave me these abilities.

BOXING

"The art of attack and defense with the fists practiced as a sport"

Muhammed Ali – Arguably the greatest heavyweight boxer of all time:

> "The fight is won or lost far away from witnesses – behind the lines, in the gym, and out on the road, long before I dance under the lights."

• • •

Carvings in wood called "relief carvings" In what is now Iraq is the earliest record of boxing dating back to over 3000 BC. In 2000 BC depictions illustrating boxers and spectators were drawn on the walls of tombs in Egypt. Boxing appeared in Greece around 7 to 8 hundred BC and found its way into the 23rd Olympics. The rules we find in a match today came about in Britain in the AD 1700. U.S.A currently holds the most Olympic gold medals with fifty. Women's boxing became a part of the Olympic program in 2012.

I do not box as one beating the air.–1 Corinthians 9:26

This is the verse I connected with the Apostle Paul as a sports fan. If Paul knew about shadow boxing as a form of training and used it in his writing, then he must have been an admirer of sports. He goes on to write, *I discipline my body and keep it under control, lest after preaching to others I myself should be disqualified.* (1 Cor 9:27) He knew that there was a time to train and a time to compete. Even though he considered himself *the least of the apostles* (1 Cor 15:9), he did not shy away from competing to *spread the fragrance of the knowledge of (Jesus) everywhere.* (2 Cor 2:14)

In any sport it takes years of training to reach a high level of competition. It is the same with the Christian life. One cannot expect constant results with wise decisions, attitudes, and integrity unless we shadowbox in our downtime. Spending quiet time with God, going to church where the Bible is taught, asking questions about God to gain more understanding, and even adding music to the playlist where the lyrics honor God are all excellent ways keep spiritual training. *Praying continually and giving thanks in all circumstances* (1 Thes 5:17,18) will definitely help. The more we train the more *in step with the Spirit* (Gal 5:25) *we become.*

Ponder: What are times and places we can spend quiet time with God?

Prayer: Father, help me dedicate to change and become more like the person I want to be.

WINNERS AND LOSERS

"Be successful or victorious in a contest or conflict"
"Be deprived or cease to have or retain a conflict or contest"

Thurman Thomas – American football running back held the record for most yards from scrimmage 4 years in a row, played for the Buffalo Bills that won the AFC 4 years in a row, yet lost the Super Bowl 4 years in a row:

> "Work hard but have a backup plan because one day it will all be over... Let go and let God"

• • •

To declare a champion there must be a competition in which a participant or team must be victorious over another. Just being the fastest, strongest, or most knowledgeable doesn't guarantee a triumph. One must endure the trials sport and overcome a variety of obstacles to win just the day. Achievements come when personal or team goals are met, whether they be more victories than the previous season, a bronze or silver metal which was introduced at the 1904 Olympics, or a gold medal or championship trophy.

> *When the thousand years are ended, Satan will be released from his prison and will come out to deceive the nations... and gather them for battle.–Revelation 20:7,8*

Throughout history there have been innumerable battles and wars. Even in the future there will be more as Jesus said, *"and you will hear of wars and rumors of wars. See that you are not alarmed, for this must take place, but the end is not yet."* (Matt 24:6) The verses in

Revelation 20:7,8 is the very last battle. Satan tries one last time to conquer God as earths authority but will be defeated and *thrown into the lake of fire. This is the second death.* *(Rev 20:14)* The God who stood victorious at the creation of everything will be the undefeated, undisputed champion in the end.

What does that mean for us? God says, *"the one who conquers will have this heritage..., but as for the cowardly, the faithless, the detestable..., and all liars, their portion will be the lake of fire."* *(Rev 21:7)* Jesus what seemed to have lost when crucified, did in fact sacrifice himself to become *victorious over sin and death* *(1 Cor 15:57)* with his resurrection. Because Jesus is who he is and did what he did, *for everyone who has been born of God overcomes the world. And this is the victory that has overcome the world -our faith.* *(1 John 5:4)* Not all will be victorious in the end though. *All the nations will be gathered before God, and He will separate them on from another, as a shepherd separates sheep from the goats.* *(Matt 25:31)* The sheep are believers in Jesus and the goats are those that rejected Jesus. The sheep will inherit the kingdom and the goats cast into the eternal fire, which is a shame because God does not *wish that any should perish.* *(Peter 2:9)*

Ponder: Trials are a testing of faith like: Illness, an accident, or a false accusation. Do you have a trial?

Are you trying to go through it alone?

Prayer: Father, help me to rely on you and the Bible to have victory of my trial.

SPECTATOR

"A person who watches an event, show, game, or other event"

Jackie Robinson – First African American Major League Baseball Player:

> "Life is not a Spectator sport. If you're going to spend your whole life in the grandstand just watching what goes on, in my opinion you're wasting your life."

• • •

There were estimated around 45,000 that attended the early Olympic games as that is what the stadium of Olympia could hold, where most events where held. As long as there was a sport to play there was somebody to watch. From kings to children, wealthy to poor, there is no discrimination when becoming a spectator. The term Spectator Sport became popular during the Victorian era of England in the early 1800's. It distinguished games someone can easily watch verses those that can't like hunting, sailing, and long distances running.

> *Therefore, since we are surrounded by such a great cloud of witnesses, let us throw off everything that hinders and the sin that easily entangles.–Hebrews 12:1*

The "therefore" in the verse above refers to the people mentioned in Hebrews chapter 11. In that chapter there is a group that lived their lives by faith. *Who through faith conquered kingdoms, enforced justice, obtained promises, stopped the mouth of lions, quenched the power of fire, escaped the edge of the sword, were made strong out of weakness, became mighty in war..., received back their dead. Some were tortured, refusing to accept release so that they might rise again to a better life.* *(Heb 11:33-35)* These witnesses bear to the truth that a life lived for God is a life well lived.

From Jesus' birth where shepherds sent by angels to see the Messiah born *(Luke 2:8-20)* to more than five hundred after his resurrection, *(1 Cor 15:5-8)* witnesses observed that Jesus was the prophesied savior of the world. Direct witnesses of his ministry, Matthew and John wrote of what they had seen. John goes on to write "*Now there where many other things that Jesus did. Were every one of them to be written, I suppose that the world itself could not contain the books that would be written.* *(John 21:25)* If we also believe in Jesus then *the Spirit himself bears witness with our spirit that we are children of God.* *(Rom 8:16)* *"I declare and saved and proclaimed..., and you are my witnesses," declares the LORD, "and I am God."* *(Isa 43:12)*

Ponder: Have you ever witnessed a miracle or blessing of God?

Prayer: Father, help me to look for your blessings and praise you when I see them.

RUNNING

"Moving legs more rapidly than walking and that for an instant both or all feet are off the ground"

Usain Bolt – the Jamaican is considered the greatest sprinter of all time, and the fastest man holds 8 Olympic gold medals and 11 World Championship gold medals:

"There are better starters than me, but I'm a strong finisher."

• • •

The origins of running would take place very soon after the origins of walking. There are cultures that have a story about a famous run to deliver news, or a warning. One in particular is believed to be the origin of the modern marathon. As the story goes, the outnumbered Greek army was able pushed back the Persian army along a coastal area. Pheidippides was dispatched from the town of Marathon and ended in Athens to announce the victory. He ran a distance of twenty-five miles. That distance was adopted into long distance races until the 1908 Olympics in London when Queen Alexandra wanted the marathon to start at Windsor Castle and end at the Stadium, 26.2 miles in all, which is used today for modern marathons.

Ahab left quickly for Jezreel. The LORD gave special strength to Elijah. He tucked his cloak into his belt and ran ahead of Ahab's chariot to Jezreel.–1 Kings 18:45,46

The race of Elijah and Ahab started in the mountain range of Mount Carmel. Though unsure where the starting point was the distance of the run ranges from 17 to 30 miles. Elijah arrived and most assuredly told the people of God's great power. Elijah is considered among greatest prophets. God did miracles through Elijah and used him to lead Israel from dark times. Yet *Elijah was a man with a nature like ours.* (James 5:17) He delt with fear for his faith, discouragement from unanswered prayer, depression, and feelings of loneliness. But Elijah endured it all and was able to say, *"I have zealously served God Almighty."* (1 Kings 19:10)

Gold medalist runner and missionary Eric Liddell once said, "God made me for a purpose, but he also made me fast. When I run, I feel his pleasure." God made us all unique. We all have a purpose. Whether it is *teaching our children* (Duet 6:7), *encouraging others to love and good works* (Heb 10:24), *preaching the gospel* (Rom 10:14), *making disciples* (Matt 28:19), or being vulnerable and weeping *with those who weep* (Rom 12:15) we need to *run with endurance* (Heb 12:1) the course God has for us. We will assuredly have problems but know that they only *help develop perseverance, and perseverance develops strength of character, and character strengthens our confident hope of salvation.* (Rom 5:3,4) So live zealously and *press on toward the goal for the prize of the upward call of God in Christ Jesus.* (Phil 3:14)

Ponder: What purpose do you think God has for you? How can you achieve that purpose?

Prayer: Father, help me endure the failures and keep focus on my purpose.

CPSIA information can be obtained
at www.ICGtesting.com
Printed in the USA
BVHW041757160223
658686BV00012B/245